ELEMENTARY

I CHING

ROBERTA PETERS

Published in 2001 by Caxton Editions
20 Bloomsbury Street
London WC1B 3JH
a member of the Caxton Publishing Group

© 2001 Caxton Publishing Group

Designed and produced for Caxton Editions
by Open Door Limited
Rutland, United Kingdom

Editing: Mary Morton
Page layout and setting: Jane Booth
Illustration: Andrew Shepherd, Art Angle
Digital Imagery © copyright 2001 Photodisc, Inc.

Title: I CHING
ISBN: 1-84067-278-1

ELEMENTARY

I CHING

ROBERTA PETERS

CAXTON EDITIONS

4   CONTENTS

CONTENTS

34   READING AND CHANGING

THE HEXAGRAMS

38   INTERPRETING THE HEXAGRAMS AND

CHANGING LINES OF THE I CHING

92   TABLE OF HEXAGRAMS

94   INDEX

INTRODUCTION TO THE I CHING

I Ching can be pronounced Eee Ching, Yee Ching or even Yee Ging depending upon which type of Chinese language is being spoken. The word Ching is nowadays taken to mean book, but it really means intelligent scroll because that is how important or wise words were noted down for posterity before the arrival of books in ancient China. The word Ye (or I as it tends to be spelled in the West) means concerning how to deal with calamity and disaster. So I Ching really means intelligent scroll concerning how to deal with calamity and disaster, but the usual translation is the Book of Changes. You will only really discover why this is known as the Book of Changes when you reach the chapter on changing lines, because the changes in question relate to the actual way that the I Ching is used rather than any changes that may be going on in a person's life.

Below: important or wise words were noted down in scrolls for posterity before the arrival of books in ancient China.

WHAT IS THE I CHING?

The I Ching is a mixture of philosophy and fortune telling, and while it is the latter that has caught the imagination of Westerners, it should really be viewed as wise words from the gods to a Chinese person who consults it. The I Ching system provides information, wisdom, virtue, warning, advice and caution. Many readings concern progress or hindrance along one's life path. It can even advise as to which direction to travel in to maximise one's potential or to minimise the chances of disaster.

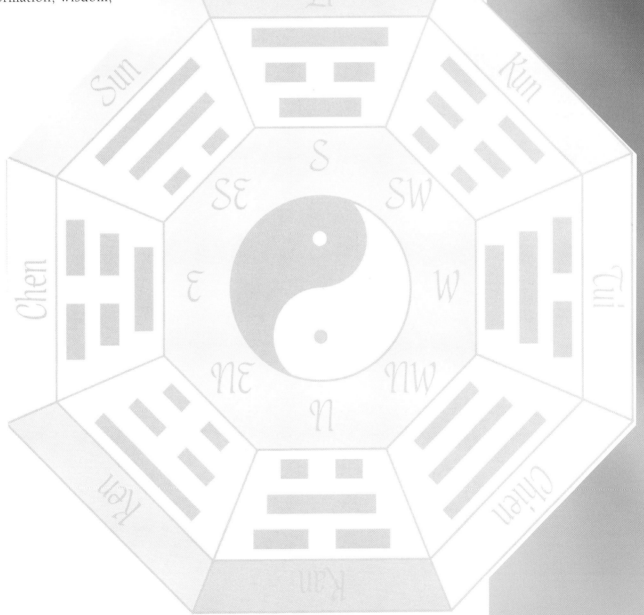

Right: In the west we are familiar with wheels of fortune (right) and gypsy fortune tellers (far right) who use various devices to look into our futures.

THE BEST APPROACH

If a Western Tarot reader, for instance, asks a client what they would like the consultant to concentrate on, the answer is invariably, "Oh, just do the reading and see what comes up." You can be sure that the client does indeed have a specific problem on their mind, but they may consider that by asking the consultant to concentrate on the one matter that is bothering them the consultant might ignore other issues. Also clients quite rightly dislike "leading" a consultant by telling them what is bothering them. It is considered to be up to the consultant to be able to work this out for themselves.

However, the I Ching is not a good vehicle for this approach. It is far better for a person to formulate a specific question and then ask the consultant to look in the I Ching book for the answer. The beauty of the system is that it doesn't actually require the services of a professional – all it needs is this book and a bit of patience.

THE HISTORY OF THE I CHING

The origins of some parts of the I Ching are incredibly ancient and they are thought to go back at least 7,000 years or more. Long ago, Oriental shamans tried to obtain answers to vexed questions by reading parts of the bodies of animals. After a goat or sheep had been sacrificed or killed for food, its shoulder blade would be roasted over a fire until a crack formed in the drying bone. In these very early divinations, a crack that formed an unbroken line was considered to be yang which would represent a positive "yes" answer to a question. A broken yin line indicated a negative "no" answer.

Far right: a Chinese temple, one of the places people go to in China to consult the I Ching.

Far left: the Emperor Fu Hsi was inspired by the sight of what he considered to be a magical animal, called a Hippogriff, which is said to have climbed out of a river and revealed the trigrams of the I Ching along its flanks.

It is the Emperor Fu Hsi who is credited with turning this original single-line interpretation into the three-line trigrams of the I Ching. He seems to have been inspired by the sight of what he considered to be a magical animal, called a Hippogriff, which is said to have climbed out of a river and revealed the trigrams of the I Ching along its flanks. The chances are that this animal was a primitive Mongolian or Siberian ass which still exists and which has faint zebra-like stripes on its flanks. Such an ass may have wandered south after a particularly bad winter. From that point forward, the I Ching utilised the three lines of the trigram rather than the single-line answer.

From this point, myths, legends and local stories began to weave themselves into the trigram readings. Eventually these turned into easily remembered verses which were then passed down by one generation of scholars after another. In the 17th century BC the verses began to be noted down on strips of bamboo. In the 12th century BC, King Wen wrote the first commentaries on the trigrams of the I Ching. King Wen then fell foul of Emperor Chou Hsin but his son, the Duke of Chou, released King Wen and restored him to his throne. Over time, King Wen, his son Tan and the Duke of Chou continued to work on the I Ching, and it is the duke who is credited with setting two trigrams atop one another to make a hexagram. In the 6th century BC Confucius and Lao Tze became interested in the system. Confucius wrote further commentaries and it was he who gave the system its name.

Right: the Duke of Chou is credited with setting two trigrams atop one another to make a hexagram.

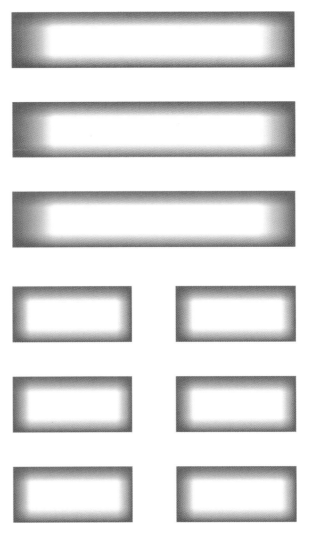

After this period, peace and stability left China for several centuries and a variety of smaller warring states came into being. Many philosophies proliferated and different versions and interpretations of the I Ching abounded. After this, the Emperor Chin unified China once again and gave it strong government. One method that he used to keep control of his subjects was to outlaw writing and some forms of knowledge, including the works of Confucius. The I Ching survived, though, passed on orally by the gypsies who had the advantage of never settling anywhere long enough to be controlled by any government.

Below: AncientChinese coins used to consult the I Ching.

During the last imperial dynasty which lasted from 1644 to 1912, the original roots of the I Ching were rediscovered and studied – and this time they remained in print. The Chinese communists disapproved of Chinese divinations, considering them to be useless superstition, but they realised that it was too late to ban them altogether. Chinese divinations have now become so universally known that even if a repressive future government banned them again, they would continue to exist in many places outside China.

Traditionally either coins or special sticks are used to find the lines that make up a design which can then be looked up in the I Ching book.

If you visit a temple in China, you will find wooden or bamboo vases with sticks in them which are kept on a shelf higher than the heads of the people who visit the temple. These are places for anyone who wishes to seek advice from the Chinese gods, either in conjunction with an I Ching book or with the help of an expert. Traditional I Ching sticks are made from a plant called yarrow or milfoil which looks a bit like cow parsley but which has very straight and sturdy stalks. Yarrow is better known as milfoil in Britain and can be found in marshy areas. When the yarrow stalks are sliced into spills and dried, they then have numbers painted on to them.

Above: Chinese coins and yarrow sticks, tools of the I Ching.

Below: A Chinese temple, where wooden or bamboo vases hold the sticks.

Yarrow sticks are usually kept in a bamboo vase on a shelf that is higher than the head. The height of the shelf keeps the sticks closer to the gods than to the mundane world below. Before consulting them, it is wise to spread a special cloth that is kept expressly for the purpose onto a clean table. This is to distinguish an I Ching reading from anything that would normally be put on a table such as food, newspapers, business articles and so on. This makes a reading into an occasion which is spiritual and special. It is then usual to light three joss sticks and to make a prayer to the gods. Three is considered to be a lucky number.

The vase is then gently shaken, allowing some of the sticks to start to slide out of it. The three sticks that protrude furthest are selected. If the sum of the numbers on the sticks is an odd number, then an unbroken line is written down on a piece of paper. If this comes to an even number, then a broken line is drawn on the paper. The vase is shaken again and the next three most prominent sticks are removed and consulted. The broken or unbroken

line is then drawn above the previous one and the following one is drawn above that and so on.

We in the West are so used to doing things in a hurry that there is a certain value in the fact that this procedure takes time. The time spent encourages quietness and a meditative frame of mind that makes the questioner more receptive to the words of the gods as given to them via the I Ching.

Far left: light three joss sticks and make a prayer to the gods before consulting the I Ching.

Most people in the Western world prefer to use coins rather than yarrow sticks, and three coins are usually used in a reading. If you have special Chinese coins, then don't allow others to play around with them but keep them in a safe place and use them only for your specific purpose. If you have no choice but to use Western coins, try to get some freshly minted ones.

The coins can be the lowest denomination that exists because their only value is the fact they are new and untouched by anyone else's "vibes". Also keep a pretty scarf or small table cloth with your coins for the express purpose of using it for your readings. If your table is dusty or dirty, clean it before putting your special cloth on to it. Light three joss sticks and hold them in both hands while bowing three times and praying to your personal god or gods for guidance. Then pick up three coins, hold them in both hands for a moment or two and concentrate on your question. Now gently throw the three coins on to the cloth. If you use Chinese coins, call the sides that are most heavily inscribed heads or yang and the other sides tails or yin. If you use Western coins, then the heads are yang and the tails are yin.

If two or three coins land yang side up, you need to draw an unbroken line on to a piece of paper, while if two or three coins land yin side up, you need to draw a broken line on to your paper. Once you have found your first line, repeat the process and draw your second line above the first, then find your third line and draw that above the second, and so on until you have either a trigram or a hexagram, depending upon which kind of reading you want.

Below: if two or three coins land yang side up, you need to draw an unbroken line on to a piece of paper, while if two or three coins land yin side up, you need to draw a broken line on to your paper.

It is always a good idea to have a question formed in your mind before starting your I Ching reading rather than just a vague desire to "see what comes up". This is because the I Ching is much more suited to answering specific questions than simply giving a vague indication of the future. Once you have your trigram or hexagram, you are ready to consult the I Ching book. The answers in any I Ching book are not altogether black and white, so you will have to use a little imagination to see what the spirits of the I Ching are telling you.

If you are simply looking for a quick-fix answer to a question, finding one hexagram and consulting the book might be enough, but if you are looking for a more rounded reading, finding a trigram first and then a hexagram or two could be better. The trigram will show you the atmosphere that prevails in your life at the time of your reading and the hexagram will tell you what is going on and what to do about it. The trigram can also be extremely useful if you need specific advice such as which direction to travel in, the time of the year that will be significant for you and even a suggestion as to a lucky colour to wear and much more. The trigram can also point out those parts of your body that might let you down in the near future. The hexagram will give specific advice and the lines of the hexagram will add further information.

If you have the kind of mind that appreciates the beauty of symbols, images and archetypes, you will love this aspect of the I Ching, but if you simply want straight answers to questions then you could find it mildly aggravating. Even so, there may be times when you want to look a little more deeply at the subject of I Ching and it is in this area that you will find the insight that you seek.

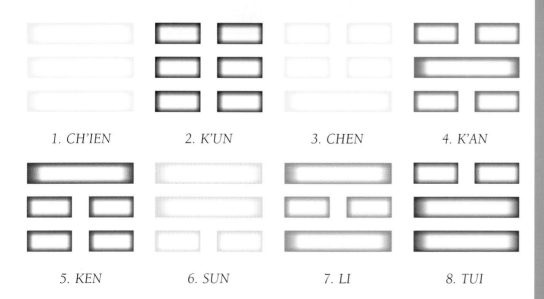

1. CH'IEN   *2. K'UN*   *3. CHEN*   *4. K'AN*

5. KEN   *6. SUN*   *7. LI*   *8. TUI*

Above: the eight trigrams of the I Ching describe the various aspects of the natural world as seen by the ancients. This is much the same as the way Western astrologers use the signs of the zodiac and planets.

SYMBOLS, IMAGES AND ARCHETYPES

An archetype is a kind of instant shorthand description – usually of a person. For example, if I were to describe someone as an earth mother you would know exactly what I mean. The same goes for whiz-kid, cowboy builder, someone with green fingers and many other simple personality sketches. To the Chinese, the positions in a family give an immediate clue as to the idea that is carried within a trigram of the I Ching. For instance, the father figure is an old-fashioned authority figure, the head of the family and the only one who is empowered to make serious decisions on behalf of the family. The mother figure also commands respect but within the home environment and only up to a certain point. Children have their place and certain natures are assigned to them – the responsible older son, the sweet-natured middle daughter, the irresponsible younger son. We all know that not all older sons are responsible, not all middle daughters are sweet natured etc., but it is the idea, the archetype, that is at work here.

The eight trigrams of the I Ching describe the various aspects of the natural world as seen by the ancients. They describe aspects of the family, parts of the body, human behaviour, directions, times of the year, colours, animal associations and much more. This is much the same as the way Western astrologers use the signs of the zodiac and planets. The trigrams vary from fully yang to fully yin and every combination between.

YANG AND YIN

You are sure to have heard of yang and yin by now but, just in case you have any doubts about these concepts, a word of explanation might be useful. The Chinese see the world as being made up of two forces or energies, both of which are necessary for balance. A surfeit of either one will create an imbalance.

Left: the familiar symbol of the yang and yin.

The yang energy is masculine, thrusting, aggressive, competitive, warlike, impatient, progressive and strong. The yin energy is feminine, enduring, conservative, nurturing, obstinate and gentle. With no yang force, nothing can progress and the world might stagnate and collapse but with no yin force, nothing can be allowed to grow and death and destruction will follow. A balance is needed. Therefore the trigrams each have their yang or yin influence which gives a clue as to which kind of energy will be needed in order to bring one's life into balance once again.

yours. Note down the number and name of the trigram next to your little drawing because you are bound to want to refer back to it later on to flesh out your later hexagram reading.

THE METHOD

The chances are that you will be using coins rather than yarrow sticks, and you will also need a pen and some paper.

Form a question in your mind and hold the coins in your hands for a moment, shake them around in your hands and then throw them on your table and look to see whether you have a majority of heads or tails. If the heads are in the majority, the bottom line will be an unbroken yang line. If tails are in the majority, you must draw a broken yin line on your note paper. Then repeat the process twice more to find the middle line and the top line.

If you happen to be using yarrow sticks, follow the instructions as per chapter 3 and then draw an unbroken yang line if your first stick number is an uneven one and a broken yin line if your first stick number is an even one. Repeat the process, drawing your second line above the first and then repeat once again placing the last line at the top.

Now check out the table of trigrams below to see which one is the same as

1. CH'IEN

Trigram name	Heaven
Family member	Father
Body parts	Head, mind, cranium
Season	Late autumn
Direction	Northwest
Nature	Strong, creative
Colour	White, gold
Plants	Chrysanthemums, herbs
Trees	Fruit trees
Animals	Horse, lion, tiger

Chi'en is one of the two most powerful trigrams. It is pure yang and extremely masculine and it represents action, drive and energy. Ch'ien represents the power of heaven or of the power that is held by the head of a family or the head of

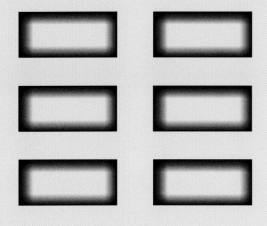

2. K'UN

Trigram name	Earth
Family member	Mother
Body parts	Stomach, abdomen, womb
Season	Late summer
Direction	Southwest
Nature	Patient, devoted
Colour	Black, dark colours
Plants	Potatoes, roots and bulbs
Trees	Trunks of trees
Animals	Ox, mare, cow, ant

an organisation. This trigram represents force, authority, strength, creativity, logic and courage. It suggests you focus your mind and your energies on a particular goal in order to achieve your particular ambition. This can refer to any kind of ambition you may have in mind. All those things that people are taught in business training sessions about goal-setting, focusing energy, believing that you can make things happen are what are needed when Ch'ien turns up. If you need to check out a particular colour or design for something that you are working on, the answer will be here.

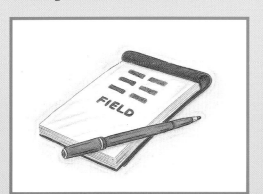

K'un is the most feminine of the trigrams and it represents the feminine attributes of care, nurture and consideration for others. K'un relates to feelings and intuition, and the key ideas are of receptivity, endurance and acceptance, docility and patience. One typically Chinese image is that of potatoes and root vegetables, because they mature in late summer and they can be stored for the winter as opposed to something fragile that must be used up immediately. The earthy image here suggests that you need to ground yourself, to be practical and not to try to deal with too many different things at once or to float around in the world of theory and abstract ideas. This trigram relates to mother figures of all kinds but it also relates to ordinary people – as opposed to important or special people.

3. CHEN

Trigram name	Thunder
Family member	Eldest son
Body parts	Foot, voice
Season	Spring
Direction	East
Nature	Strong, mobile
Colour	Yellow
Plants	Flowers, blossoms
Trees	Evergreens, blossoms, bamboo
Animals	Dragon, eagle, swallow

4. K'AN

Trigram name	Water
Family member	Middle son
Body parts	Ear, kidneys
Season	Winter
Direction	North
Nature	Dangerous, cunning
Colour	Blue
Plants	Reeds, water plants
Trees	Willow, alder
Animals	Pig, rat

Chen is associated with spring time and regeneration. After a period of drought, a thunder storm brings welcome rain, but lightning can also be destructive. This represents male arousal and sexuality, fertility, initiative, action and energy. It represents men who are young or middle-aged but not elderly. The image here is of a strong worker or leader or possibly an artist or an inventor. This would indicate a good time to make a start on something new or getting your act together in some way.

K'an represents turning points or times when one is not in control of events. Watery symbols suggest something that is hard to control, like a river which can be placid and a good means of transporting goods and people across country, but which can swell and run out of control during stormy weather. Thus K'an represents uncertainty, unpredictable times, danger and stress. If other symbols are favourable, such change is accepted as a challenge, if not then it is feared. Hard times are all around and desire is unlikely to be fulfilled for the time being. K'an represents young men, especially aggressive or difficult ones, and also fishermen. The pig and rat may not be pleasant images to Western minds, but they are both intelligent and cunning creatures who have their uses in certain situations.

5. KEN

Trigram name	*Mountain*
Family member	*Youngest son*
Body parts	*Hand, spine*
Season	*Early spring*
Direction	*Northeast*
Nature	*Still, quiet*
Colours	*Violet*
Plants	*Alpine plants*
Trees	*Nuts, olives, old trees*
Animals	*Dog, bull, leopard, mouse*

Ken represents a time of retreat and reflection when spiritual issues take precedence over worldly ones. A time when a person may forget earthly concerns and concentrate on religious or philosophical ideas, travelling on a strictly spiritual pathway for a while. The image suggestted here is of someone who seeks seclusion or who finds themself secluded, thus a priest, a monk, a prisoner and probably a sick person as well. A person who lives on a mountain and who is accustomed to seeing alpine plants and trees, for example, is behind this archetype. Ken represents male children up to the age of 16.

6. SUN

Trigram name	Wind (also Wood)
Family member	Eldest daughter
Body parts	Thigh, upper arm, lungs, nerves
Season	Early summer
Direction	Southeast
Nature	Gentle, adaptable
Colour	Green
Plants	Grass, poppies, lilies
Trees	Tall trees
Animals	Rooster, snake, tiger

7. LI (TRIGRAM)

Trigram name	Fire
Family member	Middle daughter
Body parts	Eyes, blood, heart
Season	Summer
Direction	South
Nature	Beautiful, intelligent
Colour	Orange
Plants	Tomatoes, peppers
Trees	Dried out trees
Animals	Pheasant, turtle, goldfish

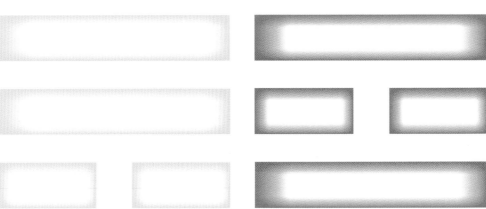

Sun represents slow growth and gradual change for the better, the gentle breezes of spring and a time of hope and renewal. Sun represents feminine virtues of endurance, gentle determination, adaptability and fair play. Sun also represents women up to middle age, those who travel, teachers and business people; it is a symbol of intelligence.

Li represents illumination and inspiration, clarity and knowledge. It is associated with young women, craftsmen and artists and those who are generous and big-hearted. Warmth and beauty are indicated here, so this would suggest a time when cultural interests and the pleasanter sides of life should be explored and enjoyed. Women might be important to the questioner at some time in the near future.

8. TUI (TRIGRAM)

Trigram name	*Lake*
Family member	*Youngest daughter*
Body parts	*Mouth, lips*
Season	*Autumn*
Direction	*West*
Nature	*Joyful, sensual*
Colour	*Red*
Plants	*Magnolia, gardenia*
Trees	*Mangrove, seaside trees*
Animals	*Sheep, birds, antelope*

Tui represents the inner psychic world and is associated with healing, magic, joy and pleasure. It links with girls under the age of 16, daughters and, oddly enough, mistresses – thus women with no real power in the family as such but who bring pleasure and fun to the all-important adult male figure.

Above: Tui represents the inner psychic world and is associated with healing, magic.

READING THE TRIGRAMS

Below: Trigrams can be an overall indication as to where your reading is going, rather like a Major Arcana Tarot card which gives an overall feel to the reading and which is then teamed with a couple of Minor Arcana cards for more clarity.

Although is it usually the hexagrams that are consulted, it may be worth finding a trigram as a kind of guide or overall indication as to where your reading is going. This can be viewed in a similar light to a Major Arcana Tarot card which gives an overall feel to the reading and which is then teamed with a couple of Minor Arcana cards for more clarity. For example, if your reading gave you the trigram, Ken, this would indicate that the best course of action is to sit back, reflect, think things over and wait upon events rather than to rush about taking action. This may also indicate that there is trouble surrounding the younger (usually male) members of your family. This would also indicate that the early spring will be an important time and that if you need to go anywhere, the northeast is the direction to take.

If your trigram was Sun, this would suggest that things are gradually changing for the better and that a time of renewal is coming. It would also indicate teaching, studying and travel on business as being good courses of action. It might suggest that you yourself are a middle-aged woman who is soon to assume some kind of good position in life or that just such a woman will soon be on hand to help you out. This would suggest that early summer will be important and that a journey to the southeast would be beneficial.

Left: the Sun Trigram indicates a change for the better and that a renewal is coming, rather like a snake shedding its skin in order to grow.

After establishing these basic facts, you should now move on to find your hexagram, your lines and then make your changes – as per the next section in this book.

READING AND CHANGING THE HEXAGRAMS

This chapter represents the nub of the I Ching and it explains why it is called the Book of Changes. It would be reasonable to think that this name refers to the fact that we consult the I Ching during times of change and uncertainty, but this is not actually the case. The changes in question refer to the way we actually use the I Ching because there are times when we swap, trade or change something for something else.

As you look through the interpretation of the hexagrams in the next chapter, you will notice that for each hexagram there is a body of text and then several numbered lines beneath it. It is logical to think that you would read the text and then go on to read the information that applies to each of the six separate lines in your hexagram, but this is not so. The fact is that one or more lines in a hexagram may be a special line, and it is these special lines that are read in addition to the main body of the text while the others are ignored. These special lines are the ones that do the changing, as we will see in a minute.

HOW TO FIND YOUR HEXAGRAM

Once you have thrown your coins and marked up your hexagram on a piece of note paper, consult the table of hexagrams below to match the pattern that you have arrived at and then note down the number of your hexagram.

HOW TO FIND YOUR SPECIAL LINES

As we have already seen in Chapter 2, you arrive at your selection of yang or yin lines as a result of the majority of your coins falling either heads or tails up when you threw them. However, when all three coins are either heads or tails, the line that is created becomes a special one. In this case, you simply mark the special line on your notepad with a cross.

It is quite possible to end up with a hexagram that has no special lines in it at all, or one that is composed entirely of special lines. The chances are that only one or two of your lines will be special ones.

After you have read through the text for your hexagram as a whole, read the text that refers to any special lines that you may have drawn. For example, if your special line is the fourth one down, read the information for line number four.

Left: when all three coins are either heads or tails, the line that is created becomes a special one.

CHANGING THE LINES

Now you can change your lines to create a new hexagram. To do this, you simply swap any special lines that happen to be unbroken yang ones for broken yin ones, and vice versa. Remember that you only swap the special lines and that you leave the remaining lines as they are. If your hexagram has no special lines then that's that – nothing changes. If your hexagram is entirely composed of special lines then the whole thing changes. The chances are that only one line or two of the lines will need to be changed.

Once you have changed a line or lines, you will, of course, have a completely new hexagram which you look up once again in the hexagram table. You read the text as a whole and then check out the line or lines that you marked as special in your first hexagram and read the same line or lines under your second hexagram, ignoring the rest.

Your first hexagram reading should give you a picture of your current situation or that which is unfolding for you in the near future and it will also offer advice on how to deal with it. The second hexagram will show you how your situation will develop. If there are no changing lines then you probably aren't going to move out of your current condition for a while yet, but if there are many changing lines, you can expect your circumstances to change radically in the near future.

You could take a view that is borrowed from the world of the Tarot which is if there is nothing of significance in your hexagram reading and no lines to change, your life and your future are in your own hands.

If your reading is a powerful one and it has more than one or two changing lines, your life is like a vehicle that is on the point of accelerating very rapidly and fate is in the driving seat. If your reading is inconclusive for some reason, try once again. If it's still inconclusive, leave the I Ching alone for a few days and then try again.

5. Look up your new hexagram in the book.

6. Read your new hexagram and see what is likely to develop out of the situation shown by your first hexagram. Read the special line under the new hexagram.

7. Leave your I Ching reading there and give yourself another one a few days later.

REVISION SECTION

Let us go over the whole affair once again in a nice logical order.

1. Create your hexagram as instructed in this book and make a note of any special lines that resulted from a throw that was all heads or all tails.

2. Read your hexagram to discover the nub of your problem and any advice that it has to offer. Perhaps put a marker in the page so that you can refer back to it later if you feel like it.

3. Read the extra little piece of information for any lines that you have marked as special. For example, if line number three is a special one read that in addition to your main hexagram. Ignore all the other lines.

4. Make your changes by swapping the special yang lines for yin lines and vice versa. This makes a completely new hexagram.

DON'T FORGET THE TRIGRAMS

Remember that you can either use the hexagrams as a stand-alone oracle or alongside a trigram reading. The trigram may tell you such things as the time of year in which you can expect your life to alter, the direction you should move towards and perhaps some other information such as the name of a tree, a flower or a colour that might have a message for you. For example, you might find a job in a place that has a blue door or you may find love in a place that is named after a particular tree or flower. To find your trigram, throw your coins three times and build up three lines from the bottom.

Although I have never read that the lines in a trigram can be made to change, there is no reason why you can't use the same technique with these as you do with hexagrams in order to see whether a new trigram emerges.

AN OPTIONAL EXTRA COMPLICATION

A second and very Chinese reason for changing lines that is absolutely unheard of in the West is to rearrange the original hexagram according to the status of the person who is having the reading. In this case, the line that represents the correct age group and status of the person is moved to the top. You will see what I mean in a moment.

1. If the questioner is a young person, a student or a trainee, leave the hexagrams in their original position.

2. If the questioner is a young person who is making headway in their job or their life, move this line to the top and move the first line to the bottom.

3. If the questioner is in their late 20s and is getting on in life, move this line to the top and move the first two lines to the bottom in their original order.

4. If the questioner is reaching middle age and/or is in middle management, move this line to the top and move the first three to the bottom in their original order.

5. If the questioner is getting on in years and/or is the head of an organisation, move this line to the top and put the first four under the bottom one in their original order.

6. If the questioner is retired, venerable, elderly and wise, move this line to the top and put all the rest underneath it in their original order.

If you want to use the system to reflect the age and status of your questioner, realign the hexagram and make a note of any special lines in their new positions so that when you read the line information and go on to change the lines, they will be the right ones.

INTERPRETING THE HEXAGRAMS
AND CHANGING LINES OF THE I CHING

Now that you have found your hexagram and made a note of any special lines, take the following steps:

Below: special lines should be changed from yang to yin or vice versa.

Check out the diagram on page 92 to find the number of your hexagram. Read your hexagram. If you have any special lines, read them and ignore the rest.

Change your special lines from yang to yin or vice versa.

Read your new hexagram including any of the lines that you have marked as special (i.e. those that have been changed).

1. CH'IEN
Creativity, creative power, the King

This hexagram is pure yang and therefore it shows masculine power at its most forceful. It doesn't take much imagination to see that the advice here is to take life by the throat and go after what you want. Initiate new methods, focus your energies and strive to reach your goals. In business, you will need to show leadership and courage and to head straight for the top. In personal life, your loved ones will turn to you for direction. The key here is to do all this without being aggressive, obstinate or nasty as bad behaviour will be sure to rebound on you later.

Top line	*Avoid over-ambition. Take things a step at a time.*
Line two	*Your thinking is clear-headed and correct.*
Line three	*Make wise choices but not necessarily the easiest ones.*
Line four	*Don't lose concentration or cease to make an effort.*
Line five	*Take advice from wiser people.*
Bottom line	*Sit back and wait a while until the picture becomes clearer.*

2. K'UN

Receptivity, responsiveness, the
Queen

This is the most feminine of the
hexagrams. This suggests that you
must use your intuition to assess
your situation and also that you go
with the flow for a while. Co-
operation is the name of the game
here and fitting in with others is what
will be needed for the time being. To
some extent your future happiness is
in the hands of others or it will
involve others so don't think only of
yourself. This emphasises the
feminine virtues of endurance, duty,
fitting in and waiting for things to
come right. Attend to practical
matters rather than to concepts,
theories and ideas. Set up workable
systems, attend to details and get
anything fixed that is broken. If you
need to buy some kind of tool or
piece of equipment, this is as good a
time as any in which to do so.

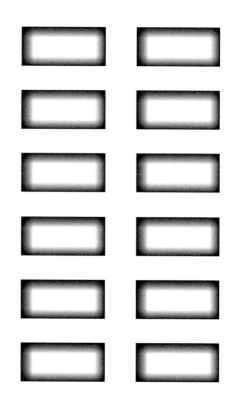

Top line	*Power struggles occur.*
Line two	*Don't boast or throw your weight around.*
Line three	*Be cautious and don't leap into anything new.*
Line four	*Don't chase fame. Be satisfied with the reputation you have.*
Line five	*Be tolerant of others and don't criticise them.*
Bottom line	*A dead loss is indicated so don't hang on to something that is sliding away.*

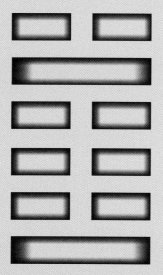

3. CHUN
Difficulty at the start

You are at the start of a new phase and you don't really know where this will take you. You need to sort through the chaos by gathering together some ideas and making a start, however confusing the picture may be. Break new ground. The implications of this as far as business matters are concerned are clear. In personal matters, take things a step at a time, remain calm and take advice if you need to. Do a few favours to others as you will need their good will in the future.

Top line	You have lost your way and you may need to find a new route.
Line two	Don't overstep the mark — keep a reasonably low profile.
Line three	Get help if you can't manage alone.
Line four	Avoid vanity, bragging or showing off.
Line five	Wait until things settle down before making new strides.
Bottom line	Stop for a while, but don't lose sight of your goal.

Below: like the dawn of a new day You are at the start of a new phase and you don't really know where this will take you.

4. MENG
Youth, folly, inexperience, learning

You need to update your skills, to gain knowledge or education or to find the information you require. Accept your ignorance and go all out to plug the gaps. Take the time to explain yourself to others. Don't try to convince others that you are clever or that you have all the answers, but be ready to listen to the wisdom of others.

Below: Meng reperesents youth, folly inexperience and learning.

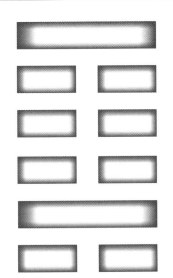

Top line	*You can't see where you are going, so stop before you trip.*
Line two	*Take things slowly and don't do anything new.*
Line three	*Don't be obsessed. Try to move on from the past.*
Line four	*Change direction now.*
Line five	*Changes are coming thick and fast now.*
Bottom line	*Humility and self-discipline are needed if you are to succeed.*

5. HSU
Waiting

This is not the time to forge ahead with anything or to force issues. You may be in a kind of limbo land with nothing much happening right now. Take advantage of this quiet period to rest and relax because you will soon be busy again. Meditate for inner wisdom and listen to the advice of sincere friends. Ambition and advancement are on the way even if they are not evident just yet. It may be beneficial to cross water soon for business or personal reasons.

Top line	Life may be hard but there are lessons to be learned from this.
Line two	Life is improving now and you should enjoy a break soon.
Line three	You are in the centre of a whirlwind. Let others fight things out between themselves and don't get involved.
Line four	Look before you leap.
Line five	Pass your wisdom on to others and inspire them.
Bottom line	Don't allow your problems to overwhelm you.

6. SUNG
Conflict

Don't try to argue your case right now because nobody is in the mood to listen. Accept criticism or a lack of credit for work done just for the moment. Don't attempt large undertakings because maintaining a steady course is the best option. Love and marriage are not favourable for the time being. Stay calm, do what you have to do, button your lip for the time being and wait for better times to come.

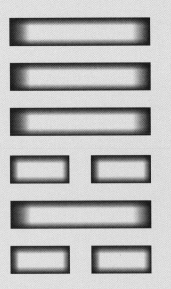

Top line	Avoid conflict if you can.
Line two	Seek out independent advice.
Line three	Give way. Don't continue to fight.
Line four	Keep your head under the parapet.
Line five	Back down.
Bottom line	Ignore gossip. Keep to the straight and narrow.

7. SHIH
The army, collective force, leadership

You have some kind of battle ahead, but somewhere around you there are forces that can be marshalled and people who will fight alongside you. You will need to maintain the confidence of those who depend upon you. Spiritual guidance is close by. You and your family may need to close ranks against injustice.

Top line	Don't fight unnecessary battles. Be honest at all times.
Line two	You are no longer in control of your situation.
Line three	Nobody seems to be in charge, so you must take over.
Line four	Look for another way around your problems.
Line five	You are on the right track, authority figures will help you.
Bottom line	Look before you leap.

8. Pi

Union, unity, joining with others

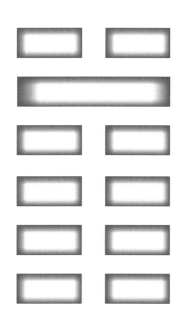

You need to join with others in some form of collective action at this time. You may need to pull together with others in a work situation or you may join a group or a team project. Perhaps it is your family that needs to stick together now. Remember to make efforts on behalf of others as well as for yourself. This is a favourable time for trust in business and also for love and marriage. This is also a good time for social activities and these may help your cause.

Top line	While everything looks good right now, trouble may be looming.
Line two	Let something go to make room for something else.
Line three	A crucial stage has been reached.
Line four	Avoid bad company or dishonest people.
Line five	Use your intuition. Follow your instincts.
Bottom line	An honest and sincere attitude will be needed.

Left: perhaps it is your family that needs to stick together now.

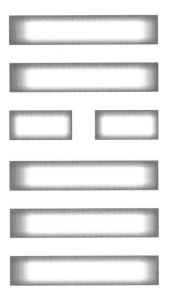

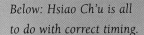

Below: Hsiao Ch'u is all to do with correct timing.

9. HSIAO CH'U
Taming small powers, restraint

This is the time to sit things out because patience and restraint will be needed. This is not a good time for large enterprises in business or to make major changes in any other area of your life either. Times may be hard for a while, but with a sensible and economic approach you will achieve your aims. If a relationship or some other situation is a total no go, walk away from it.

Top line	*Rest for a while before starting something new.*
Line two	*Collaborate with others – you can't achieve much alone.*
Line three	*Get a grip on your situation.*
Line four	*An apparent opportunity is not as good as it looks.*
Line five	*Be loyal to colleagues.*
Bottom line	*You have won the current battle – give it a rest now.*

10. LU
Caution, treading carefully

Leave things as they are until more favourable conditions apply. Be firm, even with yourself and tread the straight and narrow path. Don't allow others to take advantage of you or to force you to check your stride. Be co-operative and don't make a nuisance of yourself, but don't allow others to walk all over you either. Use your intuition.

Top line	If you have been honest and decent in the past, the future looks good.
Line two	Don't be hasty or stupid.
Line three	You are surrounded by difficulties. Keep faith in yourself.
Line four	Everything is unstable. Don't make changes now.
Line five	Keep your distance and keep your mouth shut.
Bottom line	Be independent. Don't make use of others.

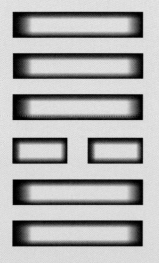

Above: Lu warns against acting too swiftly and is all to do with finding the right balance and treading a straight and narrow path.

11. T'AI

Peace, harmony, prosperity

A time of peace, harmony and happiness. Share your happiness and good fortune with those who are less well off. This is a time to plant for the future or harvest from the past. You will feel well and your career will prosper.

Top line	Bad luck is on the way. Hold things together if you can.
Line two	Be considerate towards others.
Line three	Have faith, be honest, try to get through this trying period in good heart.
Line four	Take help from others if offered, otherwise go along steadily.
Line five	Avoid gossip and also avoid getting bogged down in details.
Bottom line	You will attract nice people now.

12. P'I

Disharmony, stagnation

Poverty, loss and hard times are around you now, but a change in outlook or attitude would help. Relationships are difficult at the moment and nothing you say or do will influence matters. Just keep going and wait for better times.

Top line	The worst is over.
Line two	Make cautious changes.
Line three	If you are to blame, accept your part in the matter.
Line four	If you have been shifty in the past, you will suffer now.
Line five	Accept the current situation. Avoid bad company.
Bottom line	Hope is returning.

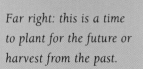

Far right: this is a time to plant for the future or harvest from the past.

13. T'UNG JEN
Community, fellowship

Teamwork is the key to success, although you may need to become the leader of the team. Competitors and battles in business will occur but there is light at the end of the tunnel. Success is yours, but you must share the benefits of this with others. Taking part in community, group or charitable activities will bring luck.

Top line	People around you are not pulling together.
Line two	Disagreement and separation.
Line three	If you have to leave, do so.
Line four	Someone around you is being selfish.
Line five	People are ganging up and you may be left out in the cold.
Bottom line	A group or partnership is falling apart.

Below: Teamwork is the key to success, although you may need to become the leader of the team.

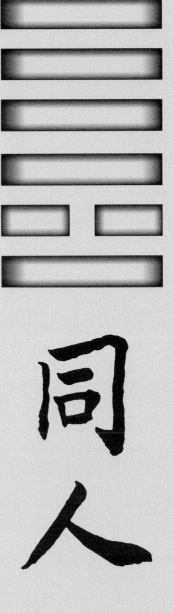

14. TA YU

Wealth, prosperity, sovereignty, plenty

A stroke of luck is on the way now. Riches, wealth and success are assured. Work and study will go together and you will soon be in a better position to understand the tasks ahead of you. Don't go overboard in trying to impress others and don't incur jealousy or resentment.

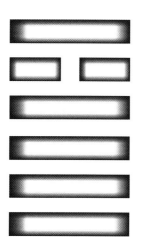

Top line	Success is assured.
Line two	Try not to antagonise others.
Line three	The rich rarely get into heaven, so be good to others while times are good for you.
Line four	Wealth and happiness are great, but don't allow them to go to your head.
Line five	Your bank balance will soon be very healthy.
Bottom line	You will soon have plenty of money, but keep some back for future rainy days.

15. CH'IEN

Modesty, moderation, the middle road

Avoid extremes and try to bring some balance into your life, especially your personal relationships. Be aware of your shortcomings and be modest and reasonable.

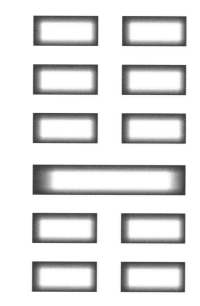

Top line	Take responsibility for your own destiny.
Line two	Be decisive and take action.
Line three	Look as if you know what you're doing, even if you don't.
Line four	People are beginning to respect you.
Line five	A change for the better.
Bottom line	Be modest and you will succeed.

16. Yu

Happiness, enthusiasm, enjoyment

A happy time is forecast with a nice balance between home life, career, social life and other matters. If you are about to embark on a new undertaking, ensure that all is in order and that there are no loose ends left hanging before you make a start. Advertise yourself and your wares to create an enthusiastic atmosphere.

Top line	Don't boast or name-drop.
Line two	Keep enthusiasm under control.
Line three	Use your enthusiasm to achieve your aims.
Line four	Steady perseverance will bring results.
Line five	Stick to your guns.
Bottom line	Don't dwell in the past. Move forward.

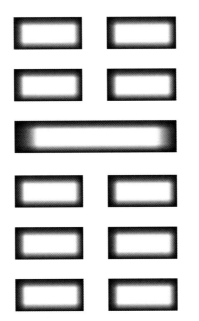

17. Sui

Following, adapting

This is a good time for marriage and personal life, but not a fortunate time for business affairs or friendship. In business it would be best to drift with the current and to allow others to show you the way or take the initiative on your behalf.

Top line	Consolidate what you have already done and teach or train others.
Line two	Stick to the path you are now on.
Line three	Be cautious.
Line four	Results will be poor.
Line five	Choices must be made.
Bottom line	Changes are afoot. Be flexible.

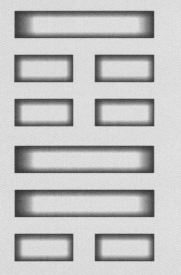

19. LIN
Approach, promotion, gathering strength

Success is assured and you will be moving ahead in your career or business now. Socially your stock will run high. Relationships will be excellent, too. It was all right in the past for you to assert yourself in order to get where you are, but now is the time to be generous to others. Remember that life is cyclical, so put something by for future rainy days.

18. KU
Repairing, clearing out decay, revising pattern

Losses, setbacks and hardship are all around. A change of attitude will help matters greatly and a change of luck is on the way. You will have to put right something that is wrong or apologise for an error or an injustice in order to correct a misunderstanding. Be scrupulously honest in all your dealings.

Top line	Great good fortune.
Line two	The future is bright.
Line three	Pursue your goals.
Line four	Continue successfully on your way.
Line five	Your star is in the ascendant.
Bottom line	Continuing as you are doing will bring good fortune.

Top line	Take some time off.
Line two	Rectify mistakes before starting something new.
Line three	Someone around you is resentful.
Line four	Make gradual changes.
Line five	Make changes but be aware of their effect on others.
Bottom line	Break old habits. Don't be rigid.

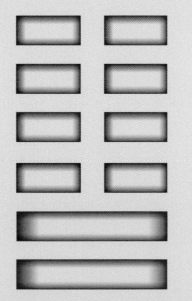

20. KUAN

Observation, contemplating, understanding

Now is the time to take up a course of study or to train for something. Learn the art of meditation and go on an inward journey in order to understand yourself. You will need to keep your eyes open for opportunities. Don't take things on trust. Be penetrative and intuitive.

Top line	Don't be egotistical.
Line two	If you are in a position of responsibility, make sure you are above reproach.
Line three	Look around you and take part in what is going on.
Line four	Look outside yourself.
Line five	Don't be self-centred. Think of others.
Bottom line	Don't blame others even if they are fools – you share some of the responsibility for errors and wrongdoing.

21. SHIH HO

Chewing, reform, biting through

Stress the positive things that you have achieved and refuse to allow others to stress the negative aspects of your life. If someone else interferes in your marriage or in a personal relationship, keep cool as they will soon lose their influence and peace will return to your household. If you have any bad habits, reform them now.

Top line	Serious trouble is brewing.
Line two	You will be punished for wrongdoing.
Line three	Serious problems are confronting you.
Line four	Change your circumstances.
Line five	Make the right choice or be prepared to fall flat on your face.
Bottom line	You have made mistakes but these are not deliberate, so you can be forgiven.

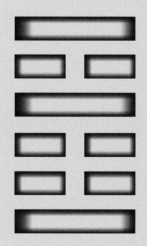

22. Pı
Gracefulness, ornament

Dress well and look successful in order to sell an idea or to promote yourself in some way. This may mean improving your appearance prior to setting out on a period of dating or socialising. Once you have accomplished your aim, don't continue to live beyond your means.

Top line	Dress well but not ostentatiously.
Line two	Give useful but inexpensive gifts.
Line three	You seem to be achieving a balance in your life now.
Line four	You can look flashy or elegant – the choice is yours.
Line five	Things are not what they look like.
Bottom line	Assess your own worth and rely upon your own good points.

Left: Dress well and look successful in order to sell an idea or to promote yourself in some way.

23. Po
Decay, instability, deterioration, disintegration

Losses and disappointments characterise this hexagram. A man may have many girlfriends, but he could soon lose his money, looks, charisma – and eventually all the girlfriends as well. This is a poor time for speculation or expansion in business.

Top line	Danger has passed – things are looking up.
Line two	The worst is over – things will improve.
Line three	Pick your friends carefully.
Line four	Don't get involved in other people's business.
Line five	Opposing forces can join for mutual benefit.
Bottom line	Things are falling apart. Stay calm.

24. Fu
Return, turning point

A change of seasons will bring improvements and a renewal of energy. Be patient. Whether it is business matters, health or relationships, improvements are on the way. Reunions are likely. Oddly enough this hexagram is not favourable for matters relating to first marriages, but it is good for subsequent ones.

Top line	You may have missed the bus.
Line two	Gains will outweigh losses.
Line three	You are striking out on your own.
Line four	Take the plunge.
Line five	Something new is on the way.
Bottom line	Retreat, think a while, then start again.

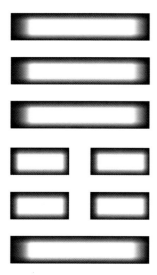

25. WU WANG

Innocence

Be honest and stay within your own limitations and allow heaven to guide you. Be unselfish and uncomplicated and don't let temporary setbacks upset you. Follow the direction given by a respected leader and good fortune will follow.

Below: Wu Wang is the hexagram of innocence.

Top line	*The end is final.*
Line two	*Misfortune follows you.*
Line three	*Trust your intuition.*
Line four	*Bad luck is on the way.*
Line five	*Do what you have to do and better times will surely come along.*
Bottom line	*Remain pure and honest and you will win through.*

26. Ta Ch'u
Taming the great powers

You will soon make great advances in your career. Hard work and steady progress will bring success. Difficulties will be overcome and even difficult people can be used to your advantage. You may get involved in politics or committees now.

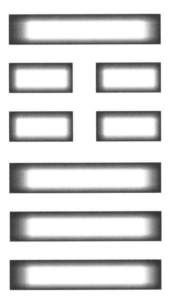

Top line	Obstacles will soon clear away.
Line two	Get to the heart of a problem and clear it away.
Line three	Your potential is good.
Line four	The way is now clear.
Line five	Back off.
Bottom line	Bide your time.

27. I
Nourishment, provision

Nourish and encourage others now. Give some thought to your loved ones and help those who work for you. This is not a time for accomplishment but for rest and relaxation.

Top line	You know what needs to be done.
Line two	You are lacking some kind of skill or piece of information.
Line three	Help others. Give to charity.
Line four	See what is real and what only looks good.
Line five	Support yourself. Stop relying upon others.
Bottom line	Don't envy others. Get out there and do it for yourself.

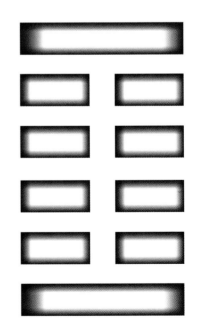

28. TA KUO

Great excess, weight, inner strength

Don't take on too much at this time. For a business person, this is a warning against too much expansion or of working too hard. Don't think of taking up with a younger lover or rescuing one with problems. If there is an escape route open to you, use it now.

大過

Left: Don't take on too much at this time.

Top line	The goal is worth accomplishing.
Line two	You are tired. Take a rest.
Line three	You can achieve a lot with help from others.
Line four	Don't be obstinate. Take a break.
Line five	Choose modest friends.
Bottom line	Be cautious when starting something new.

29. K'AN
Water, a ravine, danger

There are some nasty pitfalls ahead and a warning of danger. Don't take risks and avoid making decisions. Guard against theft, trickery and misuse of alcohol. Women will have menstrual or other female problems.

Top line	All you can do is to wait.
Line two	Go around things, not straight at them.
Line three	Be clear in your own mind about what you want to do.
Line four	The situation is out of hand.
Line five	Do what you have to do and leave major decisions for a better time.
Bottom line	If you are involved with evil people or are living a bad lifestyle, you will soon suffer the consequences.

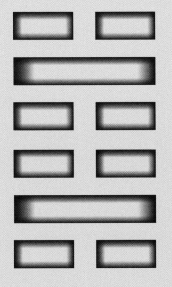

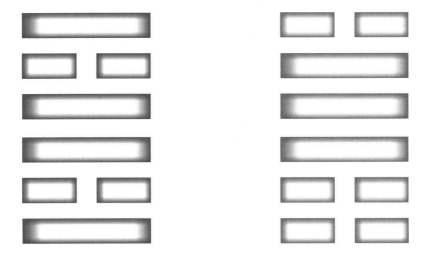

30. LI

Fire, clarity

Clear your mind and think logically and dispassionately about your life and your problems. Intellectual pursuits will go well and an intellectual approach to anything will be helpful.

Top line	Something needs to be shifted.
Line two	A reasonable attitude is needed.
Line three	What goes up must come down.
Line four	Change is inevitable.
Line five	Maintain a balanced attitude.
Bottom line	Something new is about to begin.

31. HSIEN

Attraction, relating

An attraction will bring people together and this could mean the start of a blissful love affair or a successful business partnership. Try to discover what others attract to themselves or what they want before getting too involved with them.

Top line	Don't tell me. Show me!
Line two	You may think you are being honest, but are you only being obstinate?
Line three	Someone will disagree with you.
Line four	Don't overreact.
Line five	Be patient – something will soon become clear.
Bottom line	Wait. Something good is about to happen.

咸
離

32. HENG
Duration, perseverance, enduring

Persevere and allow things to take their course because haste will bring problems. Don't insist on having things all your own way or be obstinate because a relaxed attitude would be far better.

Top line	Keep cool and take things slowly.
Line two	Apply the right amount of effort at the right time.
Line three	Your moods are unpredictable.
Line four	Be consistent.
Line five	Don't get carried away.
Bottom line	Don't try to change everything overnight.

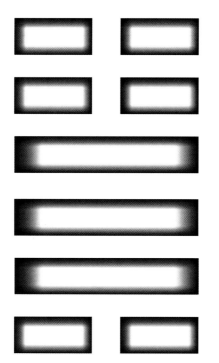

33. TUN
Retreat

Sometimes one has to step backwards before making a fresh move forwards. Business is not good now and you must not throw good money after bad. Don't embark on a love relationship or indeed anything new. There are crafty people around you who will seek to take advantage of you.

Top line	You seem to have retreated to a place of safety, so stay there for the time being.
Line two	Withdraw gracefully.
Line three	Escape from trouble and chaos now.
Line four	You are stuck in the middle of a tough situation.
Line five	Find someone to help you.
Bottom line	You are in some kind of danger now.

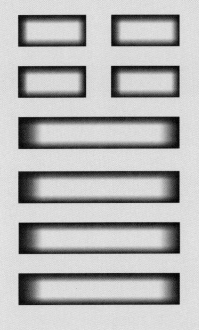

34. Ta Chuang
Great power

Take the initiative and make an effort to succeed, but don't be forceful when it isn't actually necessary. Treat lovers gently. Avoid throwing your weight around at home.

Top line	*You are at the end of the road.*
Line two	*Slow down and move forward cautiously.*
Line three	*Keep your power hidden from others.*
Line four	*Don't become arrogant.*
Line five	*You can move ahead now.*
Bottom line	*Be patient.*

Below: Ta Chuang represents great power.

35. CHIN
Progress, advancement

Your fortunes are improving and you are on the way up, so this is an excellent hexagram for business matters. Communication will be important. Don't behave aggressively.

Top line	Use a little force to get what you want.
Line two	Take on responsibilities with compassion and intelligence.
Line three	Don't be underhanded.
Line four	You can start something new, but something old has to be left behind.
Line five	A blockage in communication.
Bottom line	You can move forward slowly now.

36. MING I
Darkening of the light

When hard times arrive, be cautious and restrained but don't allow yourself to become ground down by misery. Keep your opinions to yourself and don't take on too much for a while. You will need to play your cards close to your chest and not give away secrets. A subtle approach will be needed.

Top line	Use a little force if necessary. Bad times will soon end.
Line two	You will soon be taking on extra responsibilities. Keep secrets.
Line three	Be transparently honest. Drop a project that isn't working.
Line four	A blockage will soon be removed. Change tack if necessary.
Line five	A blockage must be removed before you can progress.
Bottom line	You can't move forward yet. Keep calm and have faith.

Left: The accent will be on family life and your domestic circumstances for a while.

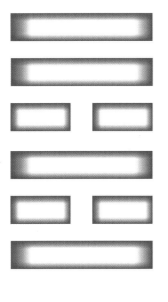

37. CHIA JEN
The family

The accent will be on family life and your domestic circumstances for a while. If you are a manager, treat your juniors as you would like to be treated. Give your superiors the deference they deserve. Keep to tradition and don't buck the system.

Top line	*Set rules for the relationship you want.*
Line two	*Don't give in to impulses.*
Line three	*A balance needs to be struck.*
Line four	*A middle path needs to be found.*
Line five	*Stick to your values and you will achieve your goals.*
Bottom line	*Be sure everyone knows what they are supposed to be doing.*

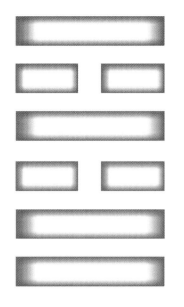

38. K'UEI
Opposition, contradiction

Don't insist that you are right, but be flexible and allow some leeway to others. Expect opposition from colleagues at work and from family members in the near future. Be co-operative and wait for this phase to pass.

Top line	Misunderstandings cause confusion.
Line two	Working with others will bring good fortune.
Line three	You will be isolated and alone.
Line four	There is a way through your problems.
Line five	Someone new will come along and sort things out for you.
Bottom line	Friendships are falling apart.

39. CHIEN
Obstruction, difficulties

If you have a problem, try to go around it rather than to moan about it or go out on a limb to solve it. Get help from others where you can. This is a bad time for practically anything and it is a particularly difficult time for love relationships.

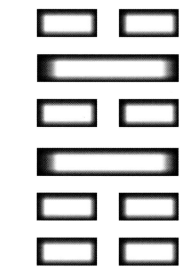

Top line	Ask for help and you will get it.
Line two	Be single-minded.
Line three	You need to ask for help.
Line four	Abandon present plans and look for a new way of doing things.
Line five	Don't run from problems.
Bottom line	Hang back and wait for better times.

40. HSIEH
Liberation

At the very worst, an acute situation will come to a head and you will know where you stand. At best, you can take action to sort your life out. Show leadership both at home and at work and don't take a rigid or inflexible stance on things.

Below: things seem like they are out of control, but you are not a tree with roots stuck in the ground. Take back control in your life and make changes to sort out the problems which stand in your way.

Top line	Give your enemies the push.
Line two	Get rid of bad habits.
Line three	Tell parasitic people to go away.
Line four	Things are out of control.
Line five	Keep alert.
Bottom line	Someone is standing in your way. Remove them.

41. SUN

Decrease

At best, you will need to redistribute some of your money or goods for the benefit of others. Perhaps a tax bill is on the way. At worst, someone will ensure that you lose some of your goods and possessions. Personal relationships will be a bit boring.

Top line	A change is as good as a rest.
Line two	Good luck is on the way.
Line three	Know your faults and do something about them.
Line four	Partnerships are good. Triangles won't work.
Line five	Fate is ruling your life now.
Bottom line	Be simple and unselfish.

42. I

Increase, benefit, the harvest

Make the most of any opportunity that comes your way, but realise that some of your success will be due to luck rather than your own cleverness. Business and finances are on the way up and love or marriage looks well starred.

Top line	You may try to give others the impression that your motives are unselfish, but they are not.
Line two	Do something good for no reward.
Line three	Use your power and position wisely.
Line four	Someone else's misfortune brings you luck.
Line five	True kindness on your part will be rewarded.
Bottom line	Success is assured. Don't be selfish.

Right: rather like the wind in the sails of a yacht, your good fortune may be due to luck rather than your own cleverness.

43. KUAI
Determination

The outlook for financial and career matters is good, but it would be worth taking out insurance policies of some kind. Don't allow bad behaviour to destroy what you have achieved. Love affairs are likely to be difficult, and quarrels will spoil the atmosphere.

Top line	*You could shoot yourself in the foot by boasting.*
Line two	*Centre yourself.*
Line three	*You are pushing something further than it wants to go.*
Line four	*You will make others angry and resentful.*
Line five	*If you must kick someone, use both feet.*
Bottom line	*A mistake now could become an insurmountable setback.*

Above: The outlook for financial and career matters is good.

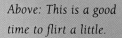

Above: This is a good time to flirt a little.

44. KOU

Encountering, temptation

This is a good time to flirt a little, to try dating a number of different people and to enjoy the social side of life, although serious commitments don't seem to be in the air right now.

Top line	*Others will think you toffee-nosed, even though you are not.*
Line two	*Don't show weakness.*
Line three	*Allow your feelings to show.*
Line four	*Fate saves you from real harm now.*
Line five	*Keep alert because both opportunities and problems are around you now.*
Bottom line	*Don't let a minor problem become a big one.*

45. Ts'ui
Gathering, assembling

You will soon meet someone who will be important to you. This could be the lover of your dreams or a good business contact. In team or work situations, harmony and the greatest effort by all concerned is what is needed.

Top line	You will try to make a relationship only to be rejected.
Line two	Follow a strong leader.
Line three	Work unselfishly for a cause.
Line four	Trouble is on the way, but this will soon be put right.
Line five	Fate brings a change for the better.
Bottom line	You may be shy, but join in group activities anyway.

46. Sheng
Ascending, advancing

If you have done the groundwork in a personal or a business situation, it will soon start to take off. Your efforts will be rewarded and creative enterprises will be successful. Avoid arrogance or over-confidence.

Top line	Don't grab a plum job out of selfish motives.
Line two	Keep your eye on the ball.
Line three	A favourable time for anything.
Line four	Find an original or unusual way of doing things.
Line five	Take things a step at a time.
Bottom line	You are on the way up.

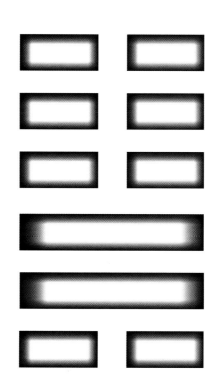

47. K'UN
Oppression, adversity

There will be hard times, probably through fate rather than your own mistakes or stupidity. Don't run away but look within yourself to find the strength to cope. Adversity can sometimes be a good thing as it brings out abilities that you don't know you have.

Top line	Don't allow past problems to colour your future.
Line two	You are bored witless. Do something new.
Line three	Don't magnify small matters.
Line four	You are bored to death. Change direction.
Line five	Give yourself something worthwhile to work for.
Bottom line	You are in a pit of despair. Don't dwell on failure or worse will follow.

Below: look within yourself to find the strength to cope

48. Ching

The well

If you have to choose between people or between paths, use your intuition and avoid those who are not straight and true. Dig deeply into yourself to find strength. Pray if necessary.

Top line	*You can move forward. Don't be afraid.*
Line two	*You may be stuck, but you can ride the situation out.*
Line three	*You can make small progress now so don't dwell on past failure.*
Line four	*You are at the bottom now, so the only way is up.*
Line five	*Use talents that you haven't bothered with for some time.*
Bottom line	*Don't over-analyse yourself or your situation – just get on and attend to practical matters.*

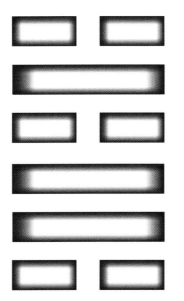

49. Ko

Revolution, change

Changes are on the way and you may move house or change your job soon. Divorce, marriage or even political changes may be in the air. Your outer manner and presentation will improve and you will soon be able to impress others.

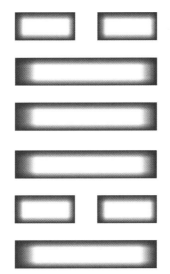

Top line	*Make small adjustments.*
Line two	*You can make changes now.*
Line three	*Selfishness and a narrow-minded attitude must be avoided.*
Line four	*Focus on your goals.*
Line five	*Make a start on something now.*
Bottom line	*Don't be impatient.*

50. TING

The cauldron

Primitive Chinese people looked after their utensils because they couldn't pop out to the shops and replace them the way we can today. The message here is to ensure that your tools, equipment and vehicles are in working order and they will look after you.

Top line	You can see things clearly now.
Line two	Success is on the way, as long as you don't throw your weight about.
Line three	Tread water now and wait for better times.
Line four	You are not using your talents properly.
Line five	Others are jealous of your success, but they aren't in a position to hurt you.
Bottom line	Success is guaranteed as long as you are not too impulsive.

Above: ensure that your tools, equipment and vehicles are in working order, whatever it is you are doing.

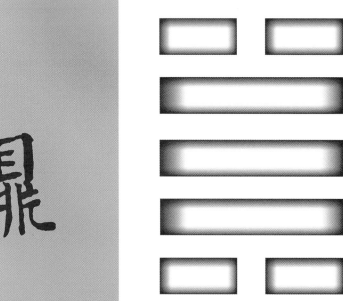

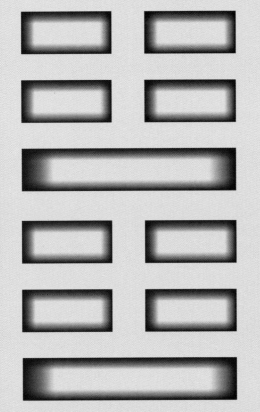

51. CHEN
Thunder, turmoil, shock

There is stormy weather ahead, but don't panic – just wait until it passes and then reassess your situation. This is good for those who communicate for a living, so expect success if you give talks and workshops or if you write or broadcast.

Top line	A shock is on the way.
Line two	Troubles, shocks and difficulties.
Line three	A shock will reduce you to immobility.
Line four	A blow of fate will poleaxe you.
Line five	A dreadful upheaval will bring great loss.
Bottom line	A dreadful time is coming to an end. There is light at the end of the tunnel.

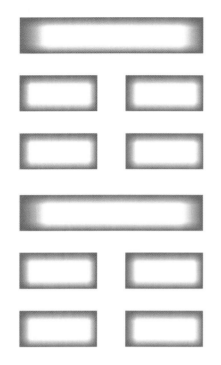

52. KEN

Stillness, keeping calm

Keep calm and don't take unnecessary gambles or take on more jobs than you are already coping with. Don't make plans – just take things a day at a time. Peace and love can be expected in the home.

Top line	*Your inner strength will help you now.*
Line two	*Centre yourself.*
Line three	*You can overcome your faults and failings now.*
Line four	*Relax and meditate.*
Line five	*Things are moving very quickly now, so go with the flow.*
Bottom line	*Maintain an objective attitude.*

Above: Keep calm and don't take unnecessary gambles or take on more jobs than you are already coping with.

53. CHIEN
Gradual development

This is a good indication of happiness in love or marriage as long as you keep to the rules. In all other things, develop slowly. Don't make sudden changes. Consolidate gains and allow life to take its course.

Top line	You must maintain the achievements you have made so far.
Line two	You have made progress, but now you must guard against mistakes.
Line three	Problems are facing you, but you can cope.
Line four	You are moving too fast. Slow down.
Line five	Friends will help you. You seem to be in a place or situation that is safe for the time being.
Bottom line	New beginnings, a fresh start.

54. KUEI MEI
The marrying girl, the maiden

We all loathe being treated with contempt, disdain and rudeness. A nasty father or mother-in-law can break up a marriage and a boss who turns his staff into victims for his own self-aggrandisement is awful. If you are a victim, don't make important decisions or flounce out of a job or a relationship prematurely. Give it time. Things might change of their own accord. Even if they don't change, you will know that you have given the situation your best shot.

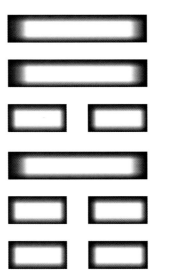

Top line	Give value for money.
Line two	Overcome vanity and pride and avoid ostentatious behaviour.
Line three	Don't take action. Sit this one out.
Line four	Compose yourself and concentrate on what you want.
Line five	Disappointment. Friends will let you down.
Bottom line	If the only job on offer is a low-grade one, take it anyway because you can always move on to better things later.

55. FENG

Greatness, prosperity, abundance, the peak

You will be happy, and trouble from outside will not harm you. Success, brilliance and prosperity are indicated, but you are warned not to over-expand or to overstep the mark. Consolidate your gains, but don't lay out money on new ventures.

Top line	You want more than you can have.
Line two	You can't solve the present problem so go around it.
Line three	Problems are passing away.
Line four	You can't win them all.
Line five	A disappointing situation.
Bottom line	Join forces with like-minded people.

Below: Feng represents Greatness, prosperity, abundance, the peak.

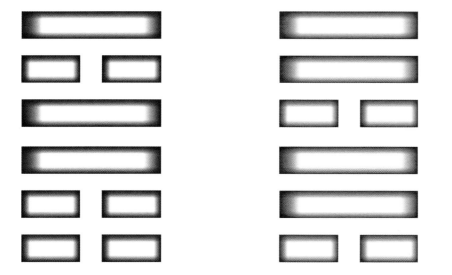

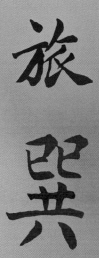

56. LU

The exile, travel

This is a good time to travel on business or pleasure and to get out and about and see what the world has to offer. You will need to market yourself soon, possibly while looking for a new job or hoping for a new relationship. Improve your manner and your appearance and be careful about whom you associate with.

Top line	Don't make a drama out of everything.
Line two	Move, travel, relocate.
Line three	Move on, travel, change tack.
Line four	Carelessness will cost you something.
Line five	Have confidence because now you can achieve success.
Bottom line	Be strong, dignified and don't put yourself down.

57. SUN

Penetration, persistence, gentleness

Keep your eye on your goal and work towards it. Travel is well starred at the moment. Be reasonable and your ideas will be accepted by others. Bend with the wind and don't be argumentative.

Top line	Knowing is not the same as doing, so do something useful.
Line two	Evaluate and re-evaluate.
Line three	Success as long as you keep your nose to the grindstone.
Line four	Think carefully and also look before you leap.
Line five	Unpleasant feelings will upset you.
Bottom line	Be firm but not hard.

Far Left: This is a good time to travel on business or pleasure and to get out and about and see what the world has to offer.

58. TUI
Joy

Careers that rely upon talking, singing, acting, teaching or diplomacy will succeed now. Inner contentment will be reflected outwardly to others. Family life should be good soon and you will have peace of mind.

Top line	Others seem to have control over your life now.
Line two	People will lead you into bad habits if you let them.
Line three	Think, then decide.
Line four	Self-indulgence and sensuality are nice but are not everything.
Line five	Weakness won't get you far.
Bottom line	Feel good about yourself, but don't grow a swelled head.

Below: Careers that rely upon talking, singing, acting, teaching or diplomacy will succeed now.

59. HUAN
Dispersion, disintegration, reuniting

A change of location is on the way. This may mean a move of house, a new venture in business, a change of job, a new car or recovery from illness. A family may be scattered and some loved ones will move on in order to improve their prospects. Marriage and relationships will be neglected for a while because you will be too busy travelling and working to concentrate on them.

Top line	Avoid dangerous situations.
Line two	An inspired idea will be useful.
Line three	Be an adjudicator or peacemaker.
Line four	The task ahead of you is great, so seek help.
Line five	Your problems are all in your own head.
Bottom line	If a quarrel is looming, sort it out now.

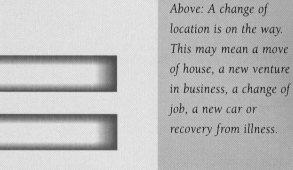

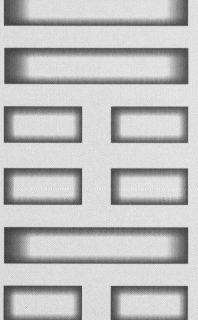

Above: A change of location is on the way. This may mean a move of house, a new venture in business, a change of job, a new car or recovery from illness.

60. CHIEH

Limitation

Teamwork and self-control will be needed. Reserves of energy, goods or money will also be needed while you sit out a difficult situation. When the doors of opportunity are once again open to you, you will be able to make your presence felt. Meanwhile, go by the rules – even if they are someone else's.

Top line	You have done your best – now wait.
Line two	You can't influence others now.
Line three	Don't be dragged into someone else's squabbles.
Line four	Concentrate on solving current problems.
Line five	A split is inevitable.
Bottom line	Take action before everything and everyone falls apart.

Above: Teamwork and self-control will be needed. Reserves of energy, goods or money will also be needed while you sit out a difficult situation.

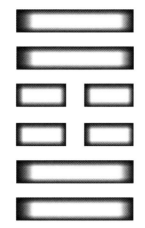

61. CHUNG FU
Inner truthfulness

Be true to yourself and sincere towards others and you will gain their trust. This hexagram predicts changes for the better in your career, business and financial matters, and especially matters of the heart. A move of house is possible and a change of scene will be beneficial.

Top line	Don't hold back. Get help if you need it.
Line two	You are in charge of the situation now.
Line three	Take advice from an authority figure.
Line four	News from those who are around you will make you happy or sad. Also the behaviour of others will affect your mood. You aren't really in control.
Line five	Insight will help you.
Bottom line	Concentrate on your good points.

Left: a move of house is possible and a change of scene will be beneficial.

62. KSIAO KUO
Slight excess, moderation

Progress will be halted, but don't allow negativity or bad feelings to stand in your way. Give generously of your time and your resources and these will be repaid. Don't waste your energy or get into a panic needlessly. If storms arrive, look for a safe perch and sit them out.

Top line	Don't overreach yourself.
Line two	Everything will go well.
Line three	You may have to move house, change location or travel on business.
Line four	Your fate rests in the hands of others.
Line five	Very good luck is on the way now.
Bottom line	Good luck will come as long as you rely upon yourself and as long as you are not selfish.

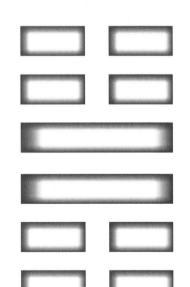

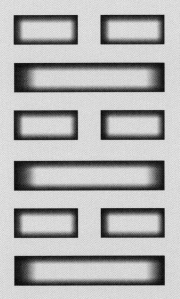

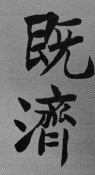

63. CHI CHI
Completion

Something has been completed and a cycle has ended. This is not the time to make further changes but to sit back and let things settle down. Guard against losing all that you have gained through behaving stupidly. Marriage or a serious relationship is favourable at this time, possibly because the courtship phase has been completed.

Top line	You may be reaching beyond your abilities.
Line two	You can make it, but you need help.
Line three	Keep your head down and get on with things.
Line four	Even if you know that you are right, don't shove this down the throats of others.
Line five	Keep your goals reasonable.
Bottom line	Don't start anything new.

Below: marriage or a serious relationship is favourable at this time, possibly because the courtship phase has been completed.

64. WEI CHI
Before completion

The previous hexagram is called completion, yet this last one is called before completion. This implies that you are almost at the end of a phase but that you may need to tie up a few loose ends before you can safely say that it is over. Clear the decks, empty your mind and get ready for something new.

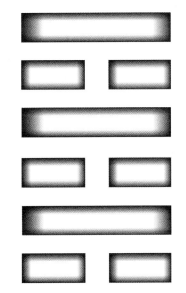

Below and Far Left: you may need to tie up a few loose ends before you can safely say that it is over. Clear the decks, empty your mind and get ready for something new.

Top line	*Celebrate, relax, enjoy your achievements.*
Line two	*You can make it if you try.*
Line three	*A struggle is inevitable, but you will overcome problems.*
Line four	*You will be frustrated for a while, so change direction if you can.*
Line five	*Patience, determination, inner faith and focusing on your goals will get you where you want to be.*
Bottom line	*Don't start anything new now. Relax and enjoy what you have achieved and give all the striving and yearning a rest for a while.*

TABLE OF HEXAGRAMS

This chart helps you locate your hexagram. When you have completed your trigrams, find your upper trigram and lower trigram and turn to the number that aligns with them both.

LOWER	Ch'ein	Chen	K'an	Ken
Ch'ein	1	34	5	26
Chen	25	51	3	27
K'an	6	40	29	4
Ken	33	62	39	52
K'un	12	16	8	23
Sun	44	32	48	18
Li	13	55	63	22
Tui	10	54	60	41

K'un	Sun	Li	Tui	
				UPPER
				LOWER
				Ch'ein
11	9	14	43	
				Chen
24	42	21	17	
				K'an
7	59	64	47	
				Ken
15	53	56	31	
				K'un
2	20	35	45	
				Sun
46	57	50	28	
				Li
36	37	30	49	
				Tui
19	61	38	58	

INDEX

INDEX